Cooking with Khalid

from 'Look North'

KHALID AZIZ

BRITISH BROADCASTING CORPORATION

Published by the
British Broadcasting Corporation
35 Marylebone High Street
London W1M 4AA

ISBN 0 563 20010 3
First published 1981
© Khalid Aziz 1981

Printed in England
by Mackays of Chatham Ltd

CONTENTS

INTRODUCTION

There is nothing new about cooking. People have been doing it virtually for ever. At first, I suppose, cooking was simply a way of making food more palatable, but over the centuries cooking has developed in many different ways to become almost an art form. These days there is no shortage of books that will give you advice on how to turn out the great classic dishes of our time, books that seem to promise that you too can be an Escoffier. Then there are the books which are designed to help harassed mums turn out tasty meals economically for their ravenous families. These books are fine in themselves, but I have always had the suspicion that there are still a great number of people who are not catered for by the average cookbook. They would simply like to be told how to cook, full stop – and in particular they would like to know how to cook foods that have a kind of mystery to them; the sort of foods one finds in high street shops which everyone assumes everyone else knows about.

The proof of this theory came one night when I did a short demonstration of how to cook and eat trout on *Look North*. The Trout and Salmon Marketing Association had been bemoaning the fact that despite the relatively low price of trout, not enough people were buying it. People were frightened of the fish, they said. So I did my demonstration and in the days and weeks that followed we were inundated with letters from people who wanted to try for themselves. There were newspaper reports that in places as far apart as Barnsley and Hull fishmongers had run out of trout, so great was the demand. A new untapped supply of would-be gourmets?

Trout is just one example of a food, at one time considered exotic, which is now freely available. There are many others. In this book, linked to the demonstrations on television, I have tried to include a broad range of foods. I hope there is not a single recipe that cannot be done well by anyone. So read on.

MUSSELS

Britain is an island. Mussels and other shellfish have always featured prominently here although at one time they were considered as simply a very useful bait with which to catch bigger fish. There are amazing stories of how wives of fishermen in places like Filey and Bridlington on the East Yorkshire coast would let themselves down on ropes over the cliffs to reach the mussels on the seashore. Then they would scramble back up their ropes and trudge home to begin the long and laborious task of opening each mussel and baiting the thousands of hooks on the long lines used by their husbands the next day. In those days the oyster was more popular for human consumption and was relatively cheap. These days oysters are beyond most people's pockets but sadly they have not been replaced, as I think they should have been, by the mussel which is both plentiful and still relatively inexpensive.

Of course one thing that puts people off, is the thought that mussels could lay them out with chronic food poisoning. It is true that if you eat a bad mussel you will certainly know it within the twelve-hour incubation period of whatever dreaded bug it is that bad mussels harbour! But with care you should be able to avoid all that. The first thing to remember when buying mussels is the time of the year. The adage 'only buy shellfish when there is an R in the month' is not a bad rule to follow. In fact it is usually pretty difficult to buy mussels after about the middle of March. The next thing to remember is that when you buy mussels they must be alive. How do you know they are alive, though, when all they seem to do is just lie there keeping themselves very much to themselves tucked away in their shiny black shells? Well the secret is just that. If they are tucked away firmly in their shells they will be alive. You might see the odd one slightly open, but if it is any kind of mussel, it will snap itself shut as soon as you touch it. If it continues to lie there all agape then throw it away. Armed with those two rules you should be able to venture out quite safely and buy your first batch of mussels. All shellfish used to be sold by the pint measure, the reason being that there were always plenty of harbourside pubs and a pint pot was usually the nearest thing to hand. To this day some dockside stalls still sell mussels in this way although fishmongers, particularly in inland city centres, sell them by the pound. It does not make much difference, a pint of mussels is a very similar quantity to a pound. A pint per person is a fairly good serving since you will inevitably have to throw some away.

Once purchased, I like to keep the mussels overnight in salted water into which I have sprinkled some oatmeal or bran. The water should be quite heavily salted – it should taste like seawater! The idea of the bran or oatmeal is to encourage the mussels to come out of their shells and feed, and in doing so expel some of the sand they will have ingested during their spell in the sea. This process is not strictly necessary but I have always found it makes the mussels somewhat tastier.

When you come to prepare the mussels for cooking, scrub them well under cold running water (a stiff nail-brush is good for this) and with a sharp knife remove their beards as best you can. Some mussels may well have barnacles attached to them but there is no need to worry too much about these; just make sure each mussel is well scrubbed and well trimmed. Now they are ready for cooking.

Moules Marinières *(Serves 2)*
This is perhaps the simplest way to cook mussels and the recipe is thought to have sprung from a traditional method used by French sailors. It takes no time at all.

2 pints mussels	*1 bayleaf*
1 medium onion	*1 tsp chopped sage leaves*
1 clove garlic	*Salt and black pepper*
2 oz butter or oil	*½ pint white wine*
2 tsp chopped chives	

Prepare the mussels in the way described above and put to one side. Peel the onion and chop it finely. Do the same with the garlic. Melt the butter in a large heavy saucepan which has a tight fitting lid. Once it has melted, gently fry the chopped onion until it is soft. Do not allow the onion to brown. Now add the garlic and the herbs and pepper. Pour in the white wine. This can be any cheap plonk, and can be a little elderly, verging on the vinegary if you like. If you want to be less extravagant you can use cider instead, but it really ought to be wine. Turn the heat up and add the mussels. Reduce the heat slightly and cover the saucepan with the tightly fitting lid . Now cook the mussels for about seven minutes, shaking the saucepan from time to time. Once cooked each mussel should have popped open with its orange flesh now peeping out from inside. Fish out the mussels with a slotted spoon, throwing away any which are not open. Transfer the mussels to a warmed serving dish and place in the oven to keep hot. Fish out the bayleaf from the remaining liquor and bring it back to the boil for about a minute. Pour the liquor over the mussels in the dish and serve straight away. The best way to present *moules marinières* is simply to put the dish in the centre of the table and encourage people to help themselves one by one. Serve with plenty of brown bread and butter and perhaps a chilled white wine. By the way, you eat them with your fingers and it is quite in order for mussel eating to be accompanied by a diverse variety of slurping sounds!

Moules au Poulette *(Serves 2)*

This is another French recipe which starts off in much the same way as *moules marinières* but then develops into what I think is a rather swish dish. It involves flaming a sauce, but do not worry about that. Even if you have never flamed anything before in your life there is always a first time to set the kitchen alight!

2 pints mussels	1 tsp chopped thyme or winter
1 medium onion	savory
1 clove garlic	Salt, black pepper
4 oz butter	$\frac{1}{2}$ pint white wine
1 bayleaf	2 tbsp brandy
2 tsp chopped chives	$\frac{1}{2}$ pint fresh double cream

Prepare the mussels for cooking in the way described above. Chop the onion finely and do the same with the garlic. Melt the butter in a large heavy saucepan and gently fry the onion until soft but do not allow it to brown. Add the garlic and fry for a further minute. Add the herbs and black pepper and then the white wine and salt. Add the mussels, increase the heat and cover the saucepan. Cook for about seven minutes shaking the saucepan from time to time. Remove the saucepan from the heat and fish out the mussels with a slotted spoon, discarding any that have remained closed. Remove the empty half shell from each mussel (you need asbestos fingers for this but persevere!) and lay the full half shells in a warmed casserole in layers. Cover the top layer of mussels with a double thickness of dampened kitchen towel. Put the casserole in a warm oven.

Now return to the liquor. Remove the bayleaf and bring the liquor back to the boil and boil rapidly for three minutes. Transfer the liquor to a frying pan and return to the boil. Now reduce the heat and stir in the fresh cream and add about half a teaspoon of freshly ground black pepper. Add the brandy; the cream will appear to curdle but continue to stir with a wooden spoon. Pull the frying pan to one side and allow the brandy to catch fire. It will flame for a few seconds as the alcohol is burned off. Stir once more and (remembering to remove the kitchen towel!) pour the sauce over the mussels in the casserole and serve immediately. When eating *moules au poulette* remember to use the half shell to scoop up as much of the sauce as possible: it is too good to waste!

Mussels Salad with Yogurt *(Serves 2)*

1 pint mussels	1 pint yogurt
1 tsp chopped chives	$\frac{1}{2}$ cucumber
1 bayleaf	2 tbsp vinegar
Salt and pepper	1 tsp paprika
$\frac{1}{2}$ pint water	

This is an interesting way of eating mussels cold. Mussels can be eaten without cooking, but I think it is advisable to cook all mussels before eating them. In any event it is a pretty skilled, not to say tough job, prising open fresh mussels: better to steam them open.

Prepare the mussels as described above. Place them in a large heavy saucepan and pour in the water along with the chives, bayleaf and shake of salt and pepper. Bring the water to the boil and cover the saucepan and cook the mussels for about seven minutes shaking the saucepan from time to time. Remove the mussels with a slotted spoon and shake off any excess liquor. With a sharp knife remove each mussel from its shell and place them to one side. Mix the yogurt with the vinegar and slice the cucumber. Stir the cucumber slices into the yogurt along with the mussels. Chill the salad for two hours before serving. Garnish with a sprinkling of paprika.

CASSEROLES

In recent years the casserole has declined in popularity, I suppose because it reminded too many people of days of privation when a good stew was the cheapest way of getting a hot, nourishing and, above all, filling meal. After the war, once food became more plentiful people turned to more exciting foods. Today, though, the casserole is enjoying a comeback, not because it is a cheap dish, but because it is the original convenience food. It does not require too much skilled preparation, you make it in one pot with all the ingredients thrown in and you can leave it to look after itself. Many people have written to me asking for suggestions on meals they can prepare and, using the marvels of modern ovens, have piping hot and ready to eat when they come in from work and are just dying for a filling meal.

Another recent development which has given casserole cooking a boost is the availability of slow-cook pots. These are heavily insulated electric casseroles which burn about as much electricity as a light bulb and over the course of several hours cook any casserole or stew to a turn. Their advantage is that you do not have to heat a whole oven just to cook the one casserole. Certainly if you live alone, one of these pots can be a great advantage.

There must be as many casserole recipes as there are ovenproof dishes and I firmly believe that you never make the same casserole twice, and neither should you. This is one area of cooking where experimentation and adaptation are a must. The following recipes, though, will give you the broad outlines, and are a good basis to follow.

Irish Stew (Serves 4)
This is very much the archetypal stew, the one which started it all. It's a pity that this dish has had generations of disservice done to it as a staple dish on the menus of canteens and school dinner halls up and down the country where, shall we say, the pursuit of gastronomy has not always won out over economics. Irish stew in itself is an economical dish

but that means one should not stint on the little extra ingredients that make it tasty. Thyme and sage for example. Do try to use fresh herbs if you can; if you cannot, use half the stated quantities below of dried herbs instead. Neck of lamb or scrag end is the traditional meat used in Irish stew. It is one of the cheaper cuts and it really is not worth putting any better cut into the stew. However, you do not want too much fat on the meat and if you can get the butcher to cut the neck into bite-size pieces, it will save you a job.

2 lb neck of lamb	*4 large potatoes*
2 large onions	*2 tsp chopped thyme*
1 tsp chopped sage	*$\frac{3}{4}$ pint meat stock*
2 tsp salt	*Pepper*

Peel the potatoes and cut them into slices about half an inch thick. Peel the onions and slice them, too, into half-inch slices. Layer the onion and potato slices together with the pieces of meat in an ovenproof casserole sprinkling in the herbs, salt and pepper as you do so. Finally, pour over the stock. Cover the casserole and cook in a moderate oven for about two hours until the meat is tender. Serve scalding hot with crusty bread. If someone does not burn their mouth you have not brought the stew to the table quickly enough!

Pork Casserole *(Serves 4–6)*
This recipe calls for pieces of diced pork. There are many pork recipes which use cheaper, fatty cuts of pork such as belly, but I feel that too much fat does not really enhance a stew, so it is better to buy, say, shoulder of pork, boned out to provide lean meat or cut your meat from pork chops or fillets.

$1\frac{1}{2}$ lb pork	*2 oz butter*
cut into one-inch cubes	*1 large onion*
3 large potatoes	*2 tbsp vinegar*
$1\frac{1}{2}$ pints chicken stock	*1 large tin tomatoes*
Salt and pepper	*1 clove garlic*

Melt the butter in the bottom of a flameproof casserole and gently fry the pork until it is sealed on all sides. You can tell that it is sealed when the meat begins to turn brown. It is important not to overcook the pork at this stage. While the pork is frying, peel and slice the onion into quarter-inch slices. Add the onion to the casserole and fry for a further minute. Peel and slice the garlic and add that too, followed by the stock. Peel the potatoes and cut them into two-inch pieces and add them, together with salt and pepper and vinegar, to the casserole. Finally add the tinned tomatoes. Cover the casserole and transfer it to a moderate oven and cook for one and a half hours. Check the potatoes and pork for tenderness and serve.

EXOTIC VEGETABLES

It is really only in the last ten years or so that we have seen high street greengrocers going in for what most people consider to be exotic vegetables, although it has to be said that what some people consider exotic others consider commonplace. As with anything else a lot depends on familiarity; if you know something well then it will hold no mystery for you. Take courgettes for example. People who have never heard of the name or its equivalent in Italian, zucchini, could understandably shy away from them. However describe them as baby marrows and suddenly everyone knows what you are talking about. In *Look North* country people are justly proud of their marrows although they tend to be grown to their full size rather than picked when they are young. In fact there are special strains of courgettes not designed to grow to marrow proportions and it is from these, rather than stunted marrow plants, that the courgettes on sale in the shops are produced. When choosing courgettes, go for bright shiny specimens with unblemished skins. If your greengrocer is one of the old-fashioned types who has no objection to your touching the vegetables, then make sure the courgettes are firm by giving them a quick squeeze. Courgettes can be cooked on their own, or with another exotic vegetable, like the aubergine.

The aubergine is often known as egg-plant, though quite why I really cannot see. I suppose it is approximately egg-shaped but who ever saw a bright purple egg? Anyway egg-plant is what it is known as. It is in some ways a strange vegetable, but cooks up well. Aubergines grow in tropical climates and have to be air freighted to reach us in peak condition as they do not have a very long 'shelf life'. Do beware when buying aubergines not to be sold any with wrinkled skin; once the outside of the vegetable loses its shine it is on the way down. Within hours the flesh will turn brown and that will be the end of your aubergine.

Another vegetable which enlightened greengrocers are pushing these days is the artichoke. There are two main types of artichoke: the Jerusalem which is a root and cooks like a potato and the globe artichoke which in my view is the more interesting of the two. Most of the globe artichokes on sale in this country are grown in Brittany, France, where you can see field upon field of these pale green plants thrusting their strange spiky heads skywards. When you buy artichokes, purchase one per person and make sure there is at least two inches of stem left on each one. This ensures that the base of the artichokes will not have dried out. Now you have bought your exotic vegetables, what about the cooking?

Courgette Fritters *(Serves 4)*
This is one of the easiest recipes; an easy introduction to courgettes. It uses a simple batter and in this way you can try them out as a vegetable to accompany any of the meals you would usually serve, substituting them for peas, perhaps.

8 courgettes	4 oz flour
1 egg	$\frac{1}{2}$ pint milk
1 tsp salt	$\frac{1}{2}$ tsp paprika
$\frac{1}{2}$ lemon	

Sift the flour, salt and paprika into a bowl and add the egg together with a little milk. With a wire whisk or fork mix well gradually adding the rest of the milk to make a creamy batter. Put the batter in the fridge for an hour to rest. Wipe over the courgettes with a clean, damp cloth. There is no need to wash them and this is not advisable as, depending on their condition, the courgettes could absorb water. In any event, they should not be allowed to stand in water. Trim the tops and tails off each courgette and cut each one cross-ways into slices between a half and quarter inch thick. Put the slices into a bowl and sprinkle with the juice from the half lemon.

When it comes to cooking there are two ways of complet-ing this recipe. You can either dip each courgette slice in the batter and deep fry them individually in hot fat, or melt some butter in a shallow frying pan and cook a kind of courgette pancake. To do this, once the pan is hot enough, pour in a little batter and immediately add a layer of courgettes. Pour over this layer some more batter and continue to cook. Repeat this until all the courgette slices are used up. Courgettes will absorb more or less batter depending on their condition and if you find there is not enough left the remaining courgette slices can just be fried in butter.

Stuffed Aubergines *(Serves 4)*
For this recipe choose large elongated aubergines rather than short stumpy ones. The long ones are far easier to deal with and make better cases for stuffing.

2 elongated aubergines	1 medium onion
1 clove garlic	1–4 oz tin mushrooms
2 oz butter	1 tsp chopped chives
$\frac{1}{2}$ tsp salt	Black pepper
6 oz grated cheese	

Take the aubergines and trim away the green leaves at the top of each vegetable. Cut each aubergine in half lengthways. Lay the halves, cut side uppermost, in a roasting tin and fill with water to just below the top of the vegetables. Cover with aluminium foil and set in a moderate oven, gas mark 4, 350°F, for twenty minutes. Remove from the oven and pour away the water. Using a dessertspoon, scoop out the flesh from each aubergine leaving a quarter to half an inch thickness of pulp in each aubergine shell. Put the scooped out aubergine pulp to one side. Peel and finely chop the onion and the garlic. Melt the butter in a frying pan and gently fry the onion and garlic for two or three minutes, stirring with a wooden spoon. Drain the brine from the tinned mushrooms and chop them coarsely. Add the pulp to the frying pan and reduce the heat slightly. Stir in the chopped mushrooms and add the chives, salt and a good sprinkling of black pepper. Put the aubergine shells back in the roasting tin (this time without water) and spoon the mixture into each shell, topping each one off with grated cheese. Any cheese can be used but I suggest good old Cheddar although if you want a really interesting taste try a blue cheese such as Stilton. Put the roasting tin back into the oven and cook for a further half an hour. Just before serving, brown the cheese under a grill. A good introduction to aubergines and you are bound to be asked to make it again.

Aubergine and Courgette Ratatouille *(Serves 4)*

A *ratatouille* is just a fancy name for a great mixture of vegetables with a few tomatoes thrown in for good measure. That is not to say though that it is an ordinary dish; far from it. It is just that I know many people have been put off either cooking it or eating it because it sounds mysterious. It is not. If you can make soup you can make *ratatouille*!

2 medium-sized aubergines	6 courgettes
1 medium onion	4 oz butter
1 clove garlic	2 tbsp tomato purée
¼ pint water	1 tsp salt
Black pepper	Juice of a lemon

Remove the green leaves from the aubergines. Cut the aubergines lengthways into halves and then again into quarters. Then cut them crossways into large pieces about one and a half inches long. Top and tail the courgettes and cut them crossways into half-inch-thick slices. Peel and slice the onion and garlic and fry them for two to three minutes in the butter. Then add the aubergines, courgettes and the juice of the lemon. Fry for a further four minutes using a wooden spoon to turn the vegetables over. Be careful when you do this not to squash the vegetable pieces. Now add the tomato purée, the salt and pepper and finally the water. Bring to the boil, reduce the heat and simmer for about thirty minutes stirring from time to time. *Ratatouille* is particularly good with lamb and pork as its sharpness brings out the flavour of the meat.

Artichokes Vinaigrette *(Serves 4)*

This is by far the most popular way of serving artichokes. It is also the simplest. It is almost exclusively served as a starter which is just as well as you do not get much nourishment out of an artichoke; you throw away more than you eat! Nonetheless they are great fun to eat and cooking them is no real problem.

4 artichokes
½ cup wine vinegar,
    slightly less of oil
    or sunflower oil
1 tsp chopped parsley

1 pint boiling water
½ clove garlic
1 pinch black pepper
1 pinch salt

Take each artichoke in turn and cut off the stem with a sharp knife flush with the bottom of the petals. Trim away the discoloured tops of the petals and rub the cut surfaces with the half lemon to prevent them from discolouring further. Put the artichokes into a large saucepan with a lid and cover with salted water. Boil for about thirty minutes. Test for tenderness by pushing the point of a knife into the base of one of the artichokes. It should go in easily. Remove the artichokes from the water with a slotted spoon and allow to drain upside down. It is not essential that the artichokes are served hot, in fact many people prefer to eat them chilled. In any event there is plenty of time to make the simple *vinaigrette*. Peel the garlic and chop infinitesimally finely. Mix with the oil, vinegar, salt, pepper and parsley and it is ready to serve. Place each artichoke on a small plate and invite your guests to spoon the vinaigrette over their artichokes.

To tackle an artichoke simply pull at one of the outer leaves and suck the flesh away from the bottom of the leaf. It is a very delicate, some would say almost imperceptible flavour, but it is well complemented by the vinaigrette. Eventually, many leaves later, you will reach the centre of the artichoke and come across the choke itself, recognised by its hairiness. Do not eat the choke, it is totally indigestible! Using a sharp knife, cut underneath the choke and remove it to reveal the artichoke heart which is the prize for which you have battled through all those leaves. The heart has much the same flavour as the leaves but it is more concentrated, and so is well worth the effort. If you get hooked on the flavour you can always go out and buy yourself a tin of artichoke hearts but it really is not quite the same thing.

TROUT

In the last ten years or so there has been a minor revolution down at the fishmongers. The bad news was that successive cod wars meant that sea-caught fish went rocketing up in price and the great traditional fish and chip meals, at one time an inexpensive way to feed the family, became almost a luxury. It was bad news for our trawlermen but good news for the growing band of fish farmers, who can turn out great numbers of fat, succulent rainbow trout literally in their back yards. Rainbow trout grow quickly and – as the fish farmers say – they are excellent converters. That is, for every pound of food they eat they put on very nearly a pound in weight. Apparently they are even better than pigs at converting food into flesh. All this has meant that while the cost of sea fish has been going up, the cost of trout in real terms has been steadily dropping. What was once considered a luxury fish is now well within the reach of everyone.

Having said all that, I know many people worry about how to cook trout and then, having cooked it, how to eat it. Like everything else it is easy when you know how!

First choose your trout. At the fishmongers trout usually come in two sizes. There are the large two and three pound fish, sometimes called salmon trout, and then there are the smaller trout usually under a pound in weight. Naturally anything to do with salmon tends to be more expensive and I think the smaller trout are tastier anyway, so buy one of these smaller trout per person. No fishmonger will admit to selling fish that is not at its freshest but you should be looking for a fish that has very firm flesh and a nice shiny skin. If you buy your fish from a fishmonger it is reasonable to expect the fish to be gutted, but if say you are presented with trout by a friendly fisherman you may have to do the job yourself.

The trout is a very compact fish which keeps its innards very neatly as you will discover. Insert the point of a sharp knife in the anus of the fish and slit the fish right along the

19

belly, up to the head. Now pull out the innards (you can do it!) You may find one of the tubes a bit reluctant to come away from the head end of the fish. If it is, simply cut it away as neatly as you can. Down the backbone of the fish you will find a dark line of clotted blood. Some people like to clean this away as well, and this is easily done by running your thumb nail along the backbone while holding the fish under a running tap. Wash the inside of the fish with plenty of cold water and shake the fish dry. When you have done this to your fish you are ready to stuff them.

Stuffed Trout *(Serves 2)*

2–3 oz butter	*2 tsp chopped parsley*
Half medium onion	*2 tsp chopped chives*
2–3 oz mushrooms	*Salt*
2 tsp chopped sage or	*Pepper*
1 tsp dry sage	*Juice of half a lemon*

Chop the onion quite finely, so no piece of onion is bigger than say a quarter of an inch. Chop the mushrooms too, but this time not so finely; the mushroom pieces should be half-inch sized. Now take the herbs and if they are fresh, chop them finely. I think no garden should be without its herb plot. We have one of those pots with different herbs growing in each opening; but do not try to grow mint in such a pot or it will make a takeover bid, forcing the others out! Dried herbs should always be looked upon as a substitute although at times (like the middle of winter) there is often little alternative. Now put the whole lot into a mixing bowl with the butter. If it is a bit hard chop it up into pieces. Squeeze in the lemon juice, being careful to avoid giving anyone the pip. Mix the whole lot together with the salt and pepper. If you are delicate you may use a spoon but I like to use my hand for this. Apart from being a very satisfying experience (and why not) the warmth from your hand helps soften the butter. When the ingredients are well mixed, take a piece of aluminium foil large enough to amply wrap one fish and lay one of the trout on it. Now stuff half of the mixture into the cavity of the trout. You will find there is more stuffing than cavity. That does not matter; just stuff it in as best you can. Now wrap the fish by folding the foil to make a parcel. Make sure each fold is doubled so as to seal in all the juices. Repeat this with the other fish and you are ready to cook the trout in the oven at gas mark 4, 350°F, for 35 to 40 minutes.

Now what about eating trout? Having transferred the trout from the foil to the plate, making sure to carry the juices with it, how do you set about it? If you look closely at the trout you will notice a line running along the side of the fish. If you cut into the fish along that line you will then be able to pare away the flesh from the top of the fish. Once you have eaten the top flesh, slide your knife under the backbone which now lies exposed and gently lift the bone away. Once you have done that, you will be able to eat the rest of the fish with no risk of getting a mouthful of bones. Easy, isn't it?

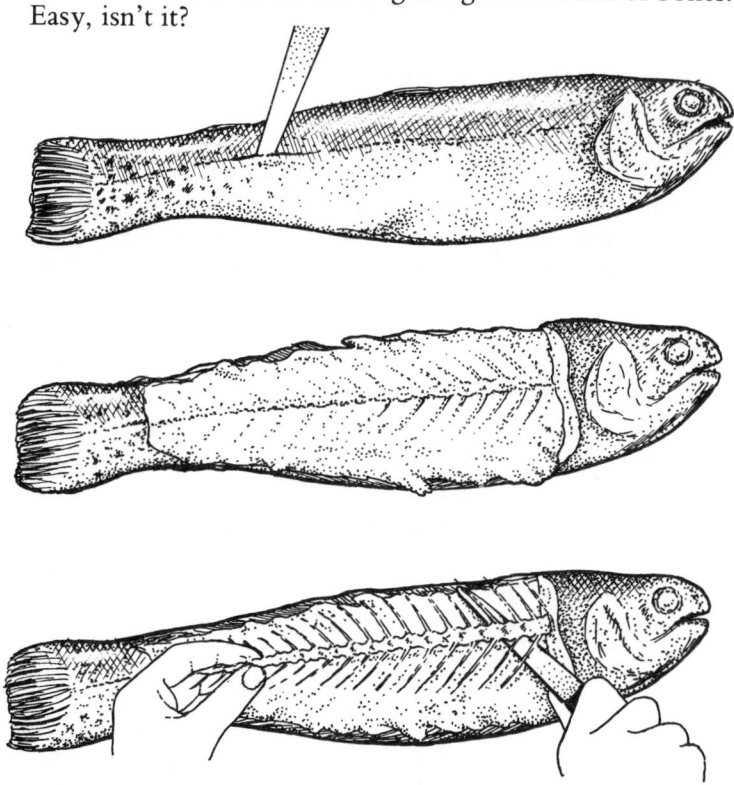

CHICKEN

These days chicken is truly a triumph of the geneticist's art, if indeed you can call it an art. These chaps have put their heads together and come up with the ideal bird, quick to grow to its full weight with the minimum consumption of food and with all the bad habits, such as feather pecking, bred out of the bird. So successful have the breeders been in producing the ideal chicken that many birds have even forgotten how to sit on eggs, as I found out to my cost when I tried to hatch chicks under birds that were originally destined for a battery farm.

All this does not sound like too much of an advertisement for the chicken industry, but it has to be said that if we expect large quantities of chicken at reasonable prices, then this is the only way found so far to achieve it. So if we can put to one side the sentimental objections we can see what great opportunities the battery bird offers us. Most people buy their chickens frozen and with the average battery bird it really does not make much difference whether it comes to you direct from the farm or frozen. The meat in my experience tastes the same. Bland. This is why it is so necessary to learn how to bring out the best in chicken by cooking it imaginatively. Some producers have even tried to help you with that, by pre-basting their birds. They do this by spraying hot butter or fat under high pressure at the birds immediately they have been plucked. The birds are then blast frozen with liquid nitrogen and the fat is held in the breast of the chicken until you come to thaw it out. The idea is that as you cook the bird the fat or butter will ooze out and save you the job of basting. Quite frankly I think it is better to baste your own chicken, rather than pay the extra for a pre-basted bird.

It is very difficult to tell the quality of anything when it is frozen rock solid so when it comes to buying your chicken you will have to be guided by the producer's good reputation. Once the bird is home you can either keep it in your freezer or prepare it straight away. Either way when it comes to thawing out the chicken you must allow enough time for it to thaw completely. This is unlikely to take less than twelve hours in the average kitchen. It is best to thaw overnight. If you try to rush it the bird will not cook properly and you will probably give yourself and your family a good dose of food poisoning – to be avoided! Once the bird is thawed out remember to remove the giblets. Usually these are in the cavity of the chicken in a plastic bag and we have all heard stories of how they are discovered just as the bird is being ceremonially carved at the table. Many people say that wiping out the chicken is good enough before roasting. I prefer to give the cavity a thorough washing out with plenty of cold water. Also check inside the cavity to ensure that there is no excess fat or skin attached to the bird.

Roasting a chicken is fairly straightfoward but many recipes call for chicken joints. You can buy joints at the butchers but I have always been doubtful about the quality of these and I think it is far better to buy a whole bird and cut it up yourself. That way you know what you are getting.

To skin and joint a chicken
First decide whether you want the chicken skinned. It is far easier to skin a whole chicken than individual joints. To skin the bird lay it the right way up and pinch the skin at the top of the breast, just above the cavity. With a knife cut the skin back towards the front of the bird, turn it over and continue the cut along the underside. What you are trying to do is remove a piece of skin about two inches wide all the way round the chicken. When you come to the parson's nose cut that off and remove the skin that comes away with it. Using a stout knife cut through the first joint on the legs of the bird and the first wing joint. There is so little meat on these that it really is not worth bothering with them. Using a damp cloth grip the remaining skin and pull it away being especially careful to pull all of the skin off the legs and wings. You should not need to cut the skin again but you might need to trim some skin from the legs.

Now to the jointing of the bird. Put the bird the right way

up and cut down into the cavity, parallel with the breast bone. Now bend the leg end back breaking the backbone. Cut through with a knife and the chicken will be in two parts. Take the legs and cut down the backbone with a sharp knife to make two joints. Stand the breast section on end and cut down the centre of the ribs. Pull the breast apart and cut down the soft bone to make two breasts. You now have four joints all roughly equal in size. You can joint the chicken further by cutting each joint in half to make eight. With most dishes this is the best thing to do and it makes it easier to serve, but if you know there are only going to be four of you to dinner then why bother!

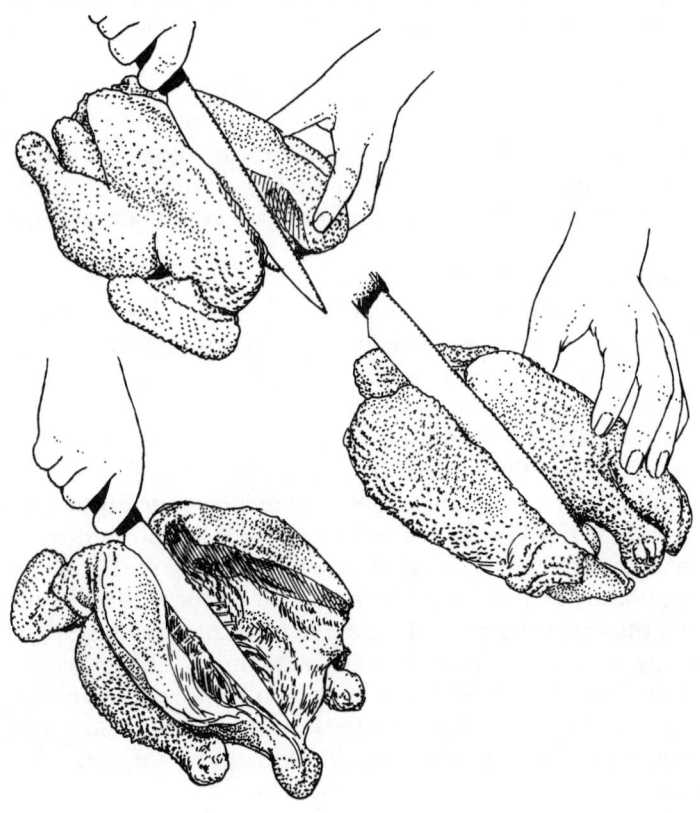

Chicken and Cashew Nuts *(Serves 4)*

On the face of it this sounds a most unlikely combination of flavours. Certainly when I first heard of it I was somewhat doubtful but after just one mouthful I was instantly converted; it really is amazing how the nuts bring out the flavour of the chicken in an almost uncanny way. One of the factors in this is, I feel, the high oil content of cashew nuts although this is helped somewhat by the addition of extra oil in the sealing process and by the addition of peanut butter. This is probably one of the easiest recipes on which to test out your newly acquired skill as a chicken jointer.

1 jointed chicken (not skinned)	2 oz oil
	1 medium onion
2 tbsp peanut butter	1 clove garlic
$\frac{1}{2}$ pint stock	$\frac{1}{4}$ pint single cream
Salt and pepper	4 oz cashew nuts

Heat the oil in a frying pan. Peel and thinly slice the onion and clove of garlic. Gently fry them for two minutes or so making sure they do not brown. Add the chicken joints, turn them to seal them on all sides. Remove the chicken joints after a further three minutes and put them to one side. Transfer the contents of the frying pan to a fireproof casserole over a flame (use an asbestos mat). If you are not sure of your casserole this next stage may be done in a heavy saucepan and then the whole transferred to the casserole. Increase the heat and add the peanut butter (the crunchy sort is best I think, but it will not ruin the dish if you go for the traditional smooth variety) together with a little of the stock. Once the peanut butter is well dissolved add the rest of the stock. Bring to the boil and boil rapidly for a good five minutes. Now add salt and pepper to taste and add the chicken pieces. Cover the casserole and place in a moderate oven (gas mark 4, 350°F). It should take just over an hour for the chicken to cook through. Just before serving stir in the cream and the cashew nuts, keeping a few to decorate.

Quick Fried Chicken *(Serves 4)*

Arguably this has become one of the fastest growing fast

foods in the West – hamburgers excepted, of course! This recipe does not make any claims about the million spices and herbs plucked from the banks of the Mississippi or suggest you should lick your fingers instead of washing them, but it does tell you how to fry chicken with little bother.

1 chicken cut into eight joints	*1 tsp chives*
skinned or unskinned	*½ tsp salt*
whichever you prefer	*½ tsp black pepper*
2 oz plain flour	*½ tsp paprika*
1 tsp thyme	*2 eggs*
1 tsp basil	*4 oz dried breadcrumbs*

Make sure the chicken joints are absolutely dry by patting them with kitchen towel. Put the flour into a large bowl and mix in the herbs, salt and peppers. This is one recipe where I think it is better to use dried herbs. If you do use fresh ones use the quantities as stated but make sure they are chopped very finely. Mix the herbs and spices well into the flour. Crack the eggs into a separate bowl and then transfer the beaten egg very carefully onto a large flat plate. Now the coating process. First roll each chicken joint in the flour making sure it is entirely covered from top to toe. Then dip it into the egg. You will see how much easier it is to do when the egg is on a flat plate. Finally roll the joint in the breadcrumbs (again on a flat plate) making sure it is thoroughly coated. Gently deep fry the joints for about ten minutes until they are golden brown. Turn out onto kitchen towel to absorb excess oil before serving.

Chicken Fricassee *(Serves 2)*
Despite its fancy name this dish is nothing more than a means of using up left over chicken – usually from a roast. There is nothing worse than a chicken which lingers on from the weekend into midweek. Your family will almost come to dread its reappearance at successive mealtimes in the guise of sandwiches and suchlike. The good thing about chicken fricassee is that once cooked, it can be instantly put in the freezer to hide for a week or two, after which it can be

pulled out as yet another blockbuster in your culinary armament!

8 oz chicken (off the bone)	*¼ pint double cream*
2 oz butter	*1 tsp chives*
Half a medium onion	*1 tsp thyme*
¼ pint chicken stock	*Salt and pepper*

When scavenging chicken from a carcase I always find it best to use my fingers to pull the meat away. If you use a knife you run the risk of cutting the meat up too small. Having pulled the meat off with your fingers you can always cut down any pieces that seem too big. This recipe calls for eight ounces of meat. It does not really matter if the amount you have is slightly more or less but do not be tempted to make up the weight with other parts of the chicken such as skin and gristle – no one will thank you if they get a mouthful of that in your otherwise delicious fricassee! Melt the butter in a large frying pan. Peel and slice the onion into fairly thin slices. Fry the onion until soft and add the chicken pieces. Fry these over a medium heat turning continuously but gently with a wooden spoon. It is important not to break up the pieces of chicken otherwise you will be left with a kind of stringy soup. It should take about four minutes to seal the chicken. Now add the stock followed by the cream – if you are feeling lavish a dash of brandy might not go amiss at this stage (in the frying pan, not you!) Season with salt and pepper to taste, add the herbs and cook for a further five to seven minutes. If you think the sauce is not thick enough turn the heat up to full and boil rapidly to reduce the volume of liquid. Allow to cool before placing in the freezer, or serve immediately. If you do freeze this dish, remember to thaw and reheat thoroughly.

Chicken Soup *(Serves 4)*

Every year when we have a turkey I swear I am going to make soup from the carcase and every year I end up not being able to face the prospect. A chicken is a different matter though – not quite so daunting. There are any number of chicken soup recipes, many of them with more vegetable than chicken in them. This recipe is simply designed to give you the basics of soup making. I am sure that very soon you will be throwing all manner of extra goodies to beef up your chicken soup (if that is quite the right way to put it).

1 chicken carcase with as much meat left on it as possible	1 tsp salt
	½ tsp chopped thyme
3 pints water	½ tsp chopped chives
2 cloves	2 oz butter
1 bayleaf	½ tbsp chopped parsley
2 medium onions	¼ pint single cream
10 whole black peppercorns	

The secret with making soup from a carcase is to prepare the carcase well. It is not simply a case of boiling it up and serving the juices you end up with. No doubt it would be nourishing enough but not particularly palatable, one of the main reasons being that it would be full of fat. So first of all remove any trace of fat and skin from the carcase. Then remove the largest pieces adhering to the carcase and put them to one side. Heat up the water in a large saucepan together with the salt, the peppercorns, cloves and bayleaf. Peel one of the onions and add that whole to the saucepan. When the water boils, slip in the carcase, reduce the heat to a simmer, cover the saucepan and cook for two and a half hours. Check the surface of the stock from time to time for fat and skim off as much of this as possible. Pour off the stock through a sieve to remove the bayleaf and pepper corns, etc. Place the stock on one side. Check the carcase for any bits of meat still adhering and cut these away and put them in the stock. Similarly any bits of chicken trapped in the sieve should be fished out and put in the stock. Melt the butter in another large saucepan. Peel and thinly slice the remaining onion and gently fry for two minutes. Now add the pieces of chicken (chopped into inch-long pieces) and fry for a further two minutes. Now add the stock, the herbs and bring to the boil. Stir in the cream and adjust the seasoning. Simmer for twenty minutes and serve.

KEBABS

I do not really know why but for some reason kebabs have always been regarded as a rather exotic import from far away. Certainly the name itself owes its origins to the Middle East but the principle is ageless. From the time the first caveman accidentally dropped some fresh meat onto his fire and discovered how much better it tasted with a burnt crust on it, the kebab was born and the kebab proper was not long to follow. Soon our caveman had learned to spear pieces of meat onto a pointed stick and cook them over his fire with some degree of control so as not to have meat dropping into the embers. That in essence is the basis of modern-day kebabs – pieces of meat on a skewer. Having said that, kebabs are very versatile and with a little imagination you can soon be creating your very own kebab recipes.

In culinary terms, kebabs took a great leap forward with the development of the marinade. A marinade is simply a sauce in which you soak your pieces of meat before cooking. It first came about as a device to counter the poor quality of meat that was generally available. Up to the turn of the century eating meat was literally a case of pot luck. Often meat would be scraggy and more likely than not going off! With the advent in modern times of public health regulations and better farming techniques, meat has improved greatly in quality. Nonetheless marinades have remained a tasty way of preparing meat.

In addition to 'purifying' the meat a marinade also serves to tenderise it. This is achieved by the acid which is an essential part of any marinade. Before you get alarmed I should say it is really only a mild acid I am talking about, found in vinegar, lemon juice or a combination of both. Such acids break down the meat fibres over a period of time and remove the toughness. There is a lot of debate over how long you need to marinate a piece of meat. It is rather like asking how long is a piece of string. It really is a matter of personal taste but in my opinion a marinade is useless if you do not leave it at least twenty-four hours, much longer for the best results. I have known people marinate meat for a fortnight but this perhaps is a little excessive and calls for a great deal of forward planning. Another point: some people say that marinades are more efficient if left at room temperature. I am sure this is true but so are all kinds of potentially harmful bacteria. I much prefer to marinate meat in a refrigerator and increase the marinading time.

When it comes to cooking kebabs much has been made of all the special attachments that do the job effortlessly for you. There was a time when no new cooker would have been complete without its rotisserie and kebab attachment. These are all very well but it is possible to produce good kebabs using an ordinary grill or, at a pinch, a combination of oven and gas cooker. Of course, if you have got a barbecue going then charcoal is ideal for kebab cooking.

A Good Basic Marinade

1 pint yogurt
¼ pint vinegar
Juice of half a lemon
2 tbsp cooking oil

1 tsp salt
1 tsp black pepper
1 medium onion
2 cloves garlic

Peel and finely slice the onion and garlic and mix in with all the other ingredients. If you have a liquidiser you will find you will be able to produce a much smoother, and therefore much more effective, marinade. This will keep for two to three weeks in a fridge and it is possible to re-use it for successive recipes calling for marinades. Use this as a base to develop your own recipes incorporating say ginger, or curry powder, or whatever else you think might go well.

Lamb Kebabs *(Serves 4)*
This dish is found in one form or another from Greece right through to China. It is the simplest to prepare and arguably the tastiest. Use flat metal skewers about two feet long. If you do not have any such skewers then strong wire can be used (coat hanger wire), but use two pieces of wire for each 'skewer' otherwise you will find the kebabs impossible to turn.

1 lb lean lamb	Salt
Basic marinade as prepared above	1 medium onion
$\frac{1}{2}$ a lemon	1 green pepper

Whilst marinades are very good for tenderising meat there is nothing they can do about fat, so trim as much fat as possible from the lamb. Now cut it into one-and-a-half-inch cubes. Take the half lemon and rub it over the meat. Now rub a little salt into each cube. Put the meat in the marinade and mix well to ensure each cube is coated on all sides. Cover the marinade and place in the fridge. Leave for two days checking from time to time that chunks of meat have not floated to the top of the marinade and exposed themselves to the air. Re-submerge any that have.

Just before you are ready to cook, peel the onion and cut it into quarters. Break each quarter up and you will be left with pieces of onion the right size to go on the skewers in between the cubes of meat. Take the green pepper, cut it in half and remove the seeds and stem and cut it into similar shapes but slightly smaller pieces. Thread the pieces of meat onto the skewers separated by the onion and green pepper. Cook either on charcoal or under a grill or in a hot oven, gas mark 6, 480°F, for ten minutes and finish off over a gas ring. Serve with rice.

Chicken Kebabs (Serves 4)

This is a very similar recipe to the one above, the main difference being that as chicken is fairly tender to start off with it need not be marinated for so long. If you make this dish it does mean you will have to learn how to remove the meat from a chicken. This is not too difficult if you follow a few simple rules. First, skin the chicken as described in the section on chicken. Using a very sharp knife remove the legs and wings of the chicken and place on one side. Do this by finding a way through the joints where they attach to the main body. Now cut away the breast meat from either side of the breast bone. Each side should be cut into two or three large pieces. Trim as much remaining meat from the body

31

as you can and then turn your attention to the legs and wings. Here the secret is to make just one cut through the flesh to the bone, along the length of the joint. Once you have done this try to ease the bone away from the flesh with a little more cutting if necessary. You should get two good pieces from each leg, one from each of the wings.

Rub the chicken pieces with the half lemon as with the lamb kebabs and then in a little salt. Marinate in the basic marinade for just twenty-four hours and then cook in the same way.

Fried Mince Kebabs *(Serves 2)*

There is a type of kebab found throughout the Middle East which is made from mince formed onto a skewer which is much thicker than those traditionally used in the West. In fact they can be three eighths of an inch across, rather like a fat knitting needle. These are rather hard to come by but this recipe gives results by frying the kebab rather than grilling it.

1 lb mince	*1 tsp salt*
1 medium onion	*1 tsp black pepper*
1 clove garlic	*2 tsp chopped parsley*
1 egg	*Juice of half a lemon*
1 tbsp breadcrumbs	

Peel the onion and cut it into quarters. Peel and thinly slice the garlic. Break up the onion and mix the pieces into the mince together with the garlic. Pass the mixture through a mincer using its finest blade. Mix in the breadcrumbs, salt, and black pepper and chopped parsley. Beat the egg and add half of it to the mince. Mix in well together with the lemon juice. Leave for two hours in a cool place. Form the mince into a cylinder an inch in diameter and three inches long. Roll each cylinder in a little of the remaining egg and fry gently until golden brown.

PASTA

Think of pasta and you think of Italy, for the Italians not only invented the dish but went on to develop it into endless forms. Pasta is the all encompassing word used to cover a whole host of dishes based on some kind of dough made up from wheat, flour and water. Sometimes pasta can be very plain or enriched with the addition of eggs and spinach. Only relatively recently has it begun to catch on in a big way in this country thanks mainly to the pizzerias opened by enterprising emigré Italians up and down the length of Britain. According to latest figures we eat about two and half pounds of pasta per head per year and if you think that sounds a lot let me tell you the Italians eat about sixty pounds per head per year.

The best known of the pastas, and probably also the one most badly done, is spaghetti, great long strands of knitting that defy you when you try to shovel them into your mouth. Sadly most people's experience of spaghetti is via a tin and that I can assure you is not the way to taste it at its best. I know many people feel a little wary of struggling home with one of those long bright blue packages of proper spaghetti but it is worth the effort and a few looks from the neighbours.

When the Italians serve pasta they invariably serve it with a sauce of some kind and so all the following recipes are for dishes with sauces apart from the spaghetti recipe itself which serves as a model for cooking all pasta. Many people now are finding it useful to serve pasta as an alternative carbohydrate to potatoes, and egg noodles which are now being widely marketed are probably as good as anything to serve in such a way; they simply require cooking like spaghetti and serving.

Spaghetti *(Serves 4)*

When you see spaghetti on sale it will probably be pre-wrapped in the bright blue paper I have described above. You will find it on offer in various lengths and really it does not matter which length you opt for as in any event you can break it up to put in the pan. The chances are you will not have an opportunity to test the spaghetti before you buy it but if you do check that it snaps cleanly. If it does not the spaghetti is soft which means it's old and won't cook well.

For four good servings you will need 1 pound of spaghetti (dry weight), a *large* saucepan and a teaspoon or two of salt.

Unwrap the spaghetti and check it over for any impurities, foreign bodies, etc. that may have got in. Stand the spaghetti upright and give it a light tap on the table to shake off any pasta dust. Fill your saucepan two-thirds full with water and bring to the boil, adding the salt. Now put the spaghetti in. Do not worry if it is too long because as soon as it starts to soften you will be able to feed the spaghetti into the saucepan. You really only break it if you have to. Continue boiling gently for about ten minutes or so. Ideally the spaghetti should be what the Italians call *al dente* which means just slightly hard in the centre of each strand. The idea is not to overcook it. Drain and serve.

When it comes to eating spaghetti everyone has his own technique. Mine is to use a spoon and fork. Twirl the fork around in the spaghetti so it picks up a few strands using the spoon for assistance and then whisk the forkful into your mouth before it all has time to change its mind and unravels. That is the theory anyway!

Bolognaise Sauce *(Serves 4)*

The essence of any good bolognaise sauce is plenty of meat in the form of minced lamb or beef and plenty of tomatoes in the form of purée and those very tasty tinned plum tomatoes. Many people make a bolognaise sauce in a saucepan but it is, I think, much easier to use a large, deep frying pan if you have one.

12 oz mince	*1–10 oz tin plum tomatoes*
4 oz cooking oil	*1 tsp oregano*
1 large onion	*½ tsp salt*
1 clove garlic	*1 tsp black pepper*
2 tbsp tomato purée	

Peel and thinly slice the onion and garlic. Fry them for four minutes in the oil. Remove and put to one side. Now add the mince to the remaining oil and fry for about five minutes, turning with a wooden spoon until the mince turns a uniform brown colour. Now add the onion together with the tomato purée. Mix this in well and add the tomatoes, but not their juice; keep this to one side. Now sprinkle in the oregano, the salt and the pepper. The oregano is essential, as this herb imparts that little something that can only be described as 'Italianness' to the dish. By now the tomatoes should be breaking up and the whole sauce taking on a uniform red colour. You are aiming for a thickish sauce. If you feel it is too thick add a little of the juice from the tinned tomatoes until the sauce reaches the correct consistency. Bring the whole back to the boil and serve instantly, poured over freshly cooked spaghetti.

Tagliatelli with Ham and Peas *(Serves 4)*

Tagliatelli is another of the myriad forms of pasta, this time it takes the shape of a long ribbon about half an inch wide drawn out and curled back on itself. It is quite freely available and in some ways is easier to manage than spaghetti.

1 lb tagliatelli	*1 small onion*
8 oz ham	*4 oz butter*
¼ pint single cream	*½ tsp oregano*
¼ pint milk	*Nutmeg*
4 oz frozen peas	*Salt and black pepper*

Cook the tagliatelli in the same way as spaghetti. Drain it and keep it warm in the oven. Prevent it from drying out by putting a piece of dampened kitchen towel over it. In a large saucepan, melt the butter. Peel and thinly slice the onion. Fry for two minutes. Take the ham and cut it into slices about half an inch wide. Sauté these with the onion for a further minute. Now pour in the cream and milk and bring to the boil. Add the peas, salt and pepper to taste and the oregano. Finally add the tagliatelli and mix well so the ham and peas are well distributed. Serve with plenty of the sauce and with a sprinkle of nutmeg to bring out the flavour.

Lasagne *(Serves 4)*

This dish is one of the few to leave the enclave of Italian restaurants and sally forth into pubs and fast food bars; the reason being it can easily be prepared and left to itself to cook. Once cooked it can be frozen and then reheated. Often this is done using microwave ovens and I am not convinced the lasagne itself tastes quite as good. Lasagne is again ribbon-shaped pasta, but this time the ribbons are much wider. Try to use lasagne verdi if you can. This is green in colour, the pasta having been mixed with spinach. Even if you do not like spinach, I still recommend you try this as it has a much enhanced flavour.

8 oz lasagne	1–10 oz tin tomatoes
4 oz oil	2 tbsp tomato purée
1 large onion	1 tsp oregano
2 cloves garlic	$\frac{1}{2}$ tsp basil
8 oz mince	Salt
4 oz mushrooms	Black pepper
2 carrots	4 oz Parmesan cheese
4 oz bacon	4 oz grated Cheddar cheese

As the lasagne comes in large sheets it is often quite difficult to keep them from breaking once they are cooked so care has to be taken. Cook in the same way as spaghetti only use about half the amount of water. You may need a bigger saucepan or have to cook the lasagne in two batches. Either way it is perhaps advisable to rub a little of the oil on each piece before cooking to prevent them sticking together. Once cooked, drain the lasagne and put on one side.

Peel and slice the onion and garlic and fry in the oil for about five minutes. Remove and put to one side and fry the mince until it is uniformly brown. Remove the mince and fry the mushrooms with the bacon (cut into small pieces). Scrape and slice the carrots into thin rings and add them to the frying pan. Now transfer everything to a large saucepan and mix all the remaining ingredients together adding salt and pepper to taste. Bring to the boil and simmer for ten minutes. Place half of this mixture in the bottom of a baking dish or casserole, and layer the cooked lasagne over it. Now add more of the mixture and another layer of lasagne and so on until it is used up. Top the whole thing off with the cheese. Bake in a moderate oven, gas mark 4, 350°F, for forty-five minutes. If by that time the cheese is not browned, place the dish under a grill for a few minutes until it is.

Macaroni Cheese *(Serves 4)*

I used to hate macaroni cheese, absolutely detest it. Much of this was I am sure due to the awful, insipid versions of it we were served at school with overcooked, watery macaroni and very little cheese. Just recently I was persuaded to put aside my childhood prejudices and try a properly made macaroni cheese. The difference was unbelievable, so it is with no hesitation that I recommend you to have a go.

8 oz macaroni	*½ tsp thyme*
½ pint milk	*½ tsp paprika*
¼ pint single cream	*1 egg*
½ tsp cornflour	*Salt and black pepper*
6 oz grated Cheddar cheese	

Cook the macaroni in the same way as spaghetti, being sure to undercook rather than overcook it. Drain and put to one side. In a large mixing bowl combine the milk, cream, thyme and paprika. Remove a little of the mixture and mix with the cornflour to form a paste and then a liquid and then return to the mixing bowl. Now mix in all but two ounces of the cheese, and the egg. Season with salt and pepper to taste and add the macaroni, mixing well. Place the mixture in a baking dish or casserole and sprinkle the remaining cheese on the top. Bake in a hot oven, gas mark 6, 400°F, for twenty minutes. Brown the cheese topping under the grill if necessary.

CURRY

Everyone has their own idea, it seems, about what a true curry is. I have heard people talk of curries to take the top of your head off with their hotness, curries that sound more like fruit salad stuffed full of sliced banana and other sweet ingredients, but I suppose the truth of the matter is that there is really no such thing as a straightforward curry. The name curry comes from the Tamil word meaning sauce and that is about as far as it goes. Nearly all so-called curries have a sauce, but there are some dry curries which have very little sauce. Curry has come to mean in this country a kind of dark brown limp stew smelling vaguely of the East courtesy of some branded curry powder and usually served on a bed of indifferent rice with a dollop of sickly sweet mango chutney in the middle. Such specimens are to be found in works canteens the length and breadth of the nation. Triumphs of culinary art they are not!

You really cannot make anything approaching an authentic curry without at least setting about it the right way, and let me stress it is the method rather than the ingredients on their own that make a curry. The basic method is very easy indeed to learn. As to the ingredients it is true that many Indian and Pakistani chefs use great long lists of spices many of which are very hard to come by in this country, but in the following recipes I have deliberately shortened the list of spices to make sure you will be able to make the dishes. It is still quite possible to produce a very passable curry despite a reduction in spices. You will see also that I have put in curry powder as one of the main ingredients. I know that many people who regard themselves as good Indian cooks shun curry powder but in India itself all cooks use a kind of curry powder, which they admittedly make themselves, called *garam masala*. I find that for simple curry cooking, curry powder provides a good base on which to build other ingredients. Of course if you use the same curry powder in the same way for all your dishes, each one of them is bound to taste the same, but with imagination there is really no limit to how useful curry powder can be.

More and more people are eating foreign food these days and certainly Indian food has been given a boost by the flurry of Tandoori restaurants that have opened in the last ten years or so. The next step is to try to produce good Indian food at home. So why not start now?

A Simple Lamb Curry *(Serves 4)*

This is very easy to cook. The only thing to be careful of is the preparation of the lamb. Do make sure you cut away all the fat as fat does not 'curry up' very well, and is extremely distasteful in a curry.

1 lb lamb	*1 tbsp curry powder*
Juice of half a lemon	*1 tsp ginger*
8 oz butter	*1 tbsp tomato purée*
2 medium onions	*2 tsp salt*
2 cloves garlic	*1 tsp black pepper*
4 cloves	*½ pint water*
4 cardamoms	

Melt half the butter in a large heavy saucepan. Cut the lamb into one-inch cubes and rub them in the lemon juice. Fry the lamb gently in the butter until it is uniformly brown and remove from the saucepan. Place the lamb to one side and add the rest of the butter to the saucepan. Peel and slice the onions and fry until they are soft. Do not allow them to brown. If you do you will end up with a dark curry with a caramel taste to it. Peel and slice the garlic and fry together with the onions. Now add the cloves. Split open the cardamoms and add both the seeds and the shells. Continue to fry gently for a further minute and then add the curry powder and ginger. Stir it in well and add the tomato purée and black pepper. Cook for a further two minutes and then add the meat, turning it over well with a wooden spoon to ensure it is well mixed in. Add water and salt; increase the heat to bring the curry to the boil. Reduce the heat to a simmer, cover the saucepan and cook for an hour. Test the meat to see whether it is cooked by pinching a piece with your fingers.

Mincemeat Curry *(Serves 4)*

This is a very popular curry in the Indian subcontinent probably because it is cheap and easy to prepare. It is often eaten as a snack in a bread roll, or used as the filling for triangular shaped patties known as samosas.

1 lb mince	$\frac{1}{2}$ tsp ginger
1 medium onion	$\frac{1}{2}$ tsp chilli powder
4 oz butter	6 oz frozen peas
1 clove garlic	$\frac{1}{2}$ tsp salt
1 tbsp curry powder	1 tsp black pepper

Melt the butter in a heavy saucepan. Peel and thinly slice the onion and garlic. Fry for about five minutes until soft. Add the curry powder, ginger and the chilli powder and fry for a further one minute. Now add the mince and cook until it is uniformly brown, turning with a wooden spoon to prevent the mince from sticking. Add the frozen peas and the salt and pepper. If the curry seems a little too dry add a drop of water. Cover the saucepan and cook over a low heat for ten minutes. This curry is supposed to have very little sauce with it and is delicious just eaten with toast.

Chicken Curry with Cream *(Serves 4)*

This is a rather opulent dish and is the kind of thing reserved for feast days. It is unheard of to cook any fowl Indian style with its skin left on, so much so that chickens are never plucked in India and Pakistan; they are skinned feathers intact! Anyway having read the chicken chapter all that holds no mystery for you!

1–3 lb chicken	$\frac{1}{2}$ tsp cinnamon
8 oz butter	1 tsp chilli powder
2 large onions	2 tsp salt
3 cloves garlic	1 tsp black pepper
10 cardamoms	5 bayleaves
10 cloves	1 pint water
2 tbsp curry powder	8 oz single cream
2 tsp turmeric	4 oz sliced almonds
1 tsp ginger	

Skin the chicken and divide it into eight joints, twelve if possible. Melt the butter in a large heavy saucepan. Peel and slice the onions and fry until soft. Add the cloves and the cardamoms (whole), stir for one minute and add the curry powder followed by the rest of the spices. Stir in well. Do not allow the heat to become too fierce during this part of the recipe. Gentle cooking is all that is needed to bring out the flavour of the spices. Now add the chicken pieces and turn them so they are well coated. Pour in the water and bring to the boil. Reduce the heat, cover the pan and simmer for two and half hours. Test the chicken for tenderness; it should almost fall off the bone when properly cooked. Add the cream and the almonds. Cook for a further ten minutes just below the boil.

Rice without tears

Any number of people have written to me over the years saying they just cannot boil rice. I hope I have been able to commiserate with them and put them on the right road to successful rice making. I certainly have the greatest of sympathy for people who find themselves unable to attempt what seems to be a simple task without ending up with a great glutinous mass. For although rice making is painfully simple you have to go about it the right way and I must confess it took me a long time to realise where I was going wrong and even now I can end up with a bad batch.

The first thing to remember is that rice is not the same across the board. There are far more varieties of rice than there are of potatoes, but for some reason many people in this country seem incapable of comprehending this fact. To them rice is something you make pudding with and when you make a rice pudding there is usually plently of liquid to stop those little grains sticking together. Having established there is more than one type of rice it has to be said that for many years we in this country were sent very inferior rice – only fit for pudding. So the first secret of making successful boiled rice is to choose the right sort. In my view Basmati is best, closely followed by one of the long grain Patna rices, many of which are hybrids developed by the Americans.

Steer clear of any rice of uncertain origin, if the person selling cannot tell you what kind it is, it is really not worth even bothering to heat the water to boil it in.

Having chosen your rice the next secret is to wash it thoroughly. Naturally you do this already, but in my experience bad washing is the cause of more congealed rice than anything else. It needs endless washing under a stream of cold running water to remove every last vestige of rice dust produced during packing and shipping. If this dust is not washed away then it will form a cellulose paste (just like wallpaper glue) and stick the grains together.

The next thing to remember is not to overcook the rice. Like pasta the cooking should stop when it is *al dente* – just a little hard in the centre of the grain. Once you reach that stage remove the saucepan from the heat and drain the rice preferably using a small-holed colander. Some people run cold water over the rice at this stage, but unless you want cold rice for a salad I do not think this is a good idea. Much better to put the rice back into the saucepan and steam off any remaining moisture over a high heat for a second or two.

When cooking rice allow one cup of dried rice per person and use just slightly more than double the quantity of slightly salted water.

GAME COOKERY

Many people have written to me saying they would love to know more about how to cook game having been very tempted by the displays of freshly killed game hung up outside shops during the winter months. The whole business of game cooking is a fascinating subject in itself, steeped in tradition. To cover it all would need at least a whole book. However there are some general pointers. First of all by game we really mean birds of the air: pheasants, partridge, pigeons, wild duck, etc., and also rabbits and hares, and occasionally deer. The selling of game is hedged around with all manner of rules and a shop needs a game licence before it is able to buy and sell game. This is all part of the ceaseless campaign against poaching which still goes on in all parts. As game has become more expensive, so poaching has become more lucrative. Two men with a long silk net can catch up to several hundred pounds' worth of partridges out in the fields by night with very little effort. Certainly the presence of so much poached game does not seem to bring the price down; the only way to do that is poach it yourself, and that is stealing!

As far as buying is concerned the game season coincides with the shooting season which starts in August (on the glorious twelfth) with grouse shooting on the moors, follows on with partridge in September, pheasants from the end of October and the whole thing comes to an abrupt end when the season finishes on 1 February. So it is a short season, some twenty weeks in all, extended perhaps by a little duck shooting and the odd hare drive. Really speaking the general availability of fresh game is between September and January.

Where do you start then when you see these beautiful creatures hanging up in fur and feather? The first thing is to plan ahead, buying pheasants should not be done on impulse. Most pheasants will be shot on a Saturday, so they are in the shops on Monday, but they will not really be ready to eat until Friday at the earliest. Which brings me to the subject of hanging game. This is the point at which many people decide they do not want to bother with game; they will buy a frozen chicken instead. The truth is so many of us have become used to meat which has not been hung that when we taste something that has it is distinctly peculiar. The prime reason for hanging is tenderness. This particularly applies to hare which if eaten the day after if has been shot will probably be rather tough. Poultry is hung unplucked and ungutted. Rabbits and hares are paunched before hanging but not skinned. The length of time you leave game to hang depends on the weather. If I am fortunate enough to come by a brace of grouse towards the end of August, then a couple of days will be sufficient as it is so much warmer. Pheasants in the depths of winter usually get about a week. There are many people who hang for much longer and those who will not hang game at all under any circumstances. In the end it depends what you prefer.

Anyway back to you casting an eye over the merchandise on display at your local purveyor of game. Having decided when you are to have your game you need to know how much to buy. As a rough guide you can reckon on a brace of pheasants (they are normally sold in pairs, a cock and a hen, which is slightly smaller) serving four people more than adequately. Allow at least one partridge per person, two quails or pigeons per person, half a duck per person, half a rabbit per person (a hare will do four, in some cases up to six people).

If you are buying game from a dealer it is reasonable to expect him to prepare it for the table. Plucking and drawing any poultry is a time-consuming and messy business and I do not really recommend it unless you have somewhere suitable to do it, like an outhouse, and a strong stomach. If you are given some game, many dealers will still dress it for you, although they are likely to make a charge for it. If you are buying game it is quite reasonable to choose, say, your pheasants on a Monday, ask for them to be hung until Thursday, plucked and drawn on Friday ready for cooking on Saturday or Sunday.

When choosing poultry check the breast of the bird for

plumpness. Check too for shot damage. Reject any bird where the leg has been broken or there is extensive bruising of the flesh (as far as you can see through all the feathers) due to the bird being shot at too close range. You have to do this at the preplucking stage; it is no use rejecting it once it has been dressed for you. Remember too that the bird has to be shot somewhere so its flesh will not be as intact as the day it was born! When it comes to rabbits and hares, shooting people make every effort to shoot them in the head. This is ideal as none of the flesh is damaged, but with the best will in the world some are going to be shot elsewhere. Guard against any shot in the legs as you could end up with finely splintered bones. When buying pheasants always ask for the best half-a-dozen tail feathers to garnish the finished dish.

Roast Pheasant *(Serves 4)*
This is still by far the most popular way of presenting pheasants at the table, and is probably the best way of introducing the birds to your family, as roasted pheasants look like slightly undersized chickens, although there the similarity ends. The taste of these birds which have had the best free ranging of all, in the wild, is just so much better.

1 brace pheasants	*1 tbsp chopped parsley*
4 oz fat bacon	*2 oz butter*
2 tbsp chopped chives	*Salt*
1 tbsp chopped thyme	*Black pepper*

Wipe out the inside of each bird. Sit the birds upright, breasts uppermost and using cocktail sticks secure strips of bacon over the breast of each bird. This is done because the flesh of pheasant tends to be rather dry. This is true of most game birds (with the exception of ducks and geese); being wild they tend to be leaner than domesticated poultry. Now take the herbs and mix them together. Divide the herb mixture and put it inside each cavity. Lay the pheasants, breasts down, each on its own sheet of aluminium cooking foil. Season each bird with salt and pepper. Melt the butter and brush it onto each bird. Seal up the cooking foil and put the pheasants in a moderate oven (gas mark 4, 350°F) and

45

cook for half an hour. Then turn the birds the right way up and re-secure the bacon. Using a pastry brush baste each bird with its juices. The idea of starting the birds off the wrong way up is again to prevent too much drying of the breast meat. After a further half hour check to see if the pheasants are thoroughly cooked by piercing the flesh with a sharp knife. When the juices run out clear the birds are cooked. Draw the foil to one side and remove the bacon. Rebaste the breast of each bird and increase the oven temperature to gas mark 6, 400°F. Cook for a further ten minutes to brown.

Serve as you would any roast with potatoes and vegetables or with a salad. Garnish the serving dish with tail feathers. You can either carve the pheasants as you would a chicken or using a pair of strong kitchen scissors cut each bird lengthways into halves and serve half a pheasant to each person. Either way I am sure you will agree that roast pheasant is a good alternative for Sunday lunch and special occasions.

Roast Quail with Grapes *(Serves 4)*

The smaller game birds such as partridge and quail can be roasted, but because of their size they tend to dry up and the results are not, in my view, very satisfactory. Far better to cook them in some kind of casserole where you can add plenty of liquid and there is no danger of the birds drying out. Whilst we are on the subject of adding liquid there seems to be a tradition in game cookery of adding plenty of alcohol to the recipes. Certainly there is plenty in the next one which comes to me from Christopher Powell, who together with his partner produces quail on Humberside. This recipe could be used to cook pigeons although it is perhaps a little opulent for so lowly a bird!

2 brace quail
3 to 4 dozen Muscat grapes
  (can be bought tinned)
6 tbsp port
¼ pint beef stock

3 oz toasted breadcrumbs
½ tsp arrowroot
Salt
Black pepper

Wipe out the insides of each quail. Take about a dozen grapes and mix together with the breadcrumbs and a little of the port, to make a firm mixture. Stuff each bird with this mixture and lay them in a casserole. Mix together the remaining port and stock and spoon about nine tablespoons of the mixture over the quail. Cover loosely with foil and cook in a moderate oven, gas mark 4, 350°F, for forty minutes. Drain off the juices into a saucepan and add the rest of the port and stock and the grapes. Mix up the arrowroot with a little of the mixture and add, stirring slowly over a medium heat. Add salt and pepper to taste. Continue to cook gently until the sauce thickens. Pour the sauce over the quail and serve. One quail per person is sufficient in this recipe.

Jugged Hare *(Serves 6)*
Rabbits and hares are, I think, only just beginning to come back into their own in this country. This is for two reasons. Firstly, myxomatosis meant that in vast areas the wild rabbit population was all but wiped out and secondly there seems to be a prejudice against eating rabbits either because of the *Watership Down* type connections or because people regard them as poor man's meat. As far as poor man's meat is concerned this could not be further from the truth. In fact rabbits are bred commercially in this country for export to the French meat markets where rabbit flesh is regarded very highly, and they should know. The relative unpopularity of rabbit and hare has meant it is still fairly inexpensive compared to feathered game. The following recipe uses hare but you could quite easily substitute a couple of rabbits and slightly reduce the cooking time. If you use hare it really is essential to see that it has been hung for a few days as it will make all the difference to the tenderness of the final dish.

Arrange to have your hare skinned and offered to you with its head removed (it will already have been paunched before hanging). You can if you like also have the hare cut into six or eight joints, if not you can do this yourself by cutting across the backbone so the hare is divided into three or four sections and then dividing up the leg joints.

1 hare	8 oz mushrooms
2 oz plain flour	2 bayleaves
1 tsp salt	1 tsp chopped thyme
1 tsp black pepper	1 tsp chopped parsley
1 tsp paprika	1 tsp chopped basil
4 oz butter	$\frac{1}{2}$ pint beef stock
4 oz bacon	$\frac{1}{2}$ pint red wine
8 oz pickling onions	1 large glass port

Sieve the flour together with the salt, black pepper and paprika. Sprinkle this seasoned flour onto a flat plate and coat each joint thoroughly, being sure to shake off any excess flour. In a large casserole melt the butter and gently fry the hare joints for about ten minutes until they are brown on all sides. Remove the joints and place on one side. Take the bacon (this can be one of the cheaper fattier cuts) and chop it into pieces not larger than an inch. Fry for about four minutes. All the frying can be done in a large heatproof casserole. That way you save having to transfer the ingredients during the cooking process. If you do not have a suitable casserole, use an ordinary frying pan for the first sections of the recipe. While the bacon is frying, peel the pickling onions and then add them to the casserole. Fry for a further two to three minutes and add the mushrooms. Button mushrooms are best for this dish but if they are not available then large mushrooms may be used cut up into strips rather than chopped. Fry the mushrooms for a further one minute tossing them with a wooden spoon. Now sprinkle in the herbs. Turn up the heat and add the beef stock and the wine and port. Bring to the boil and add the hare joints. Cover the casserole, place in a cool oven, gas mark 3, 325°F, to cook for about two hours. Test for tenderness by pinching the flesh on one of the joints to see if it is ready to come off the bone. Slow cooking is the key to successful jugged hare. Serve with potatoes and boiled cabbage. If you want to pre-prepare this dish follow the recipe up to the point where you bring the casserole to the boil.

SIMPLE STARTERS

The true function of a starter is, in a way, rather unclear. I suppose they really serve to pad out a meal and give it a little more importance than just some everyday repast. In some restaurants starters are given fancy names but in reality they are just starters and so should hold no mystery for anyone. A good starter ought to be something that lets the stomach in gently for a meal ahead. That means it should be light, tasty, but in no way should it usurp the main course in importance. Too often I have been served with an excellent starter only to be followed by a rather mediocre main course. It is no use starting with smoked salmon and following with fish and chips! Starters can be very complicated to make – sometimes more complicated than the main course itself, but most people find themselves falling back on the three old favourites which almost make themselves. They are cheap to buy, too, and always acceptable. The three favourites are grapefruit, melon and avocado.

Of the three, the first two are, I think, somewhat overworked as starters. That is not to say they should not be used, but a discerning host or hostess will attempt to add a little extra something just to pep them up and make them different to the starters served up at hotel catered functions. Avocado is a different matter. There are still great numbers of people who have yet to taste this delightfully refreshing fruit with its smooth savouriness. If I had a choice I would serve avocado in preference to melon and grapefruit every time – it is just as easy to prepare. Having said that there is still a place for the old favourites and the following recipes will give you an insight into how to improve them.

Many people these days in effect serve a starter with drinks. Instead of the usual bowls of peanuts and crisps, why not lay out a number of dips with fresh vegetables such as celery and carrots cut up into strips to dip in? Much healthier, and that way you can skip the starter at table and go straight to the main course which makes for less formality and more time spent by you with your guests.

Melon with Ginger Sauce *(Serves 4)*

When choosing melons do try to test for ripeness yourself, do not just take the fruiterer's word for it. You do this by pressing with your thumbs at the pointed ends of the melon. If there is a little give, the melon is ripe. If it feels hard look for another one. There is a French saying which goes 'Men are like melons, you have to go through ten of them to find a good one'.

1 ripe melon	*2 tsp ginger*
2 tbsp golden syrup	*1 tsp cinnamon*
1 oz butter	*1 glass white wine*

Cut the melon lengthways into four or six wedges. Remove the seeds and reform the melon securing it with a couple of rubber bands. Place in fridge to cool. Reforming the melon prevents it from drying out – there is nothing worse than dried-up melon. Melt the butter in a small saucepan and keeping the heat very low add the ginger and cinnamon. Stir for about two minutes and add the golden syrup. A trick when dealing with golden syrup, honey, or any other such thick stuff is to warm the spoon in a gas flame before attempting to spoon the liquid from the container. Stir in the syrup making sure it is well mixed with the butter mixture. Increase the heat slightly and gradually add the white wine until it is well mixed in. This sauce, which is liberally poured over the melon, can be served hot or cold. Just before serving the melon it is best to pre-cut each wedge so your guests have a sporting chance of tackling their melon. Another point, always lay out a fork in addition to a spoon when serving melon; better still lay out a knife and fork and forget the spoon altogether.

Caramel Grapefruit *(Serves 4)*

You usually run into grapefruit either at breakfast in English boarding houses or as a starter at a down-market dinner held in some anonymous plastic hotel. I always have a terrible sinking feeling when I go into the banqueting room to be confronted by serried ranks of grapefruit halves each topped with its vivid half cherry – the only culinary input in evidence apart from cutting the grapefruit in half. It is so unnecessary; with just a little more effort it could be so much better.

When buying grapefruit choose firm ones; any which have taken on a kind of dimpled appearance are on the way out. When it comes to size go for medium. The small ones are no good to man nor beast and no one wants to struggle through half a football as a starter!

2 grapefruit	*2 tbsp rum*
4 oz brown sugar	*½ tsp cinnamon*

Cut the grapefruit in half. Prepare each half for eating by cutting close to the skin all around the grapefruit to free the flesh. I am not a great believer in gadgets but I strongly suggest you invest in a grapefruit knife with its curved blade and serrated edge. Next cut radially from the centre of each half to divide the flesh into segments. Sprinkle each half with brown sugar and cinnamon and place the grapefruit under the grill for about four minutes. Be sure the edge of the peel does not burn as this looks very unsightly. If it does, then cut it away before serving. Under the grill the sugar will melt and caramelise giving a rather special flavour to the grapefruit. You should serve them straight from the grill sprinkled with the rum (dark rum is best). Please, please, please resist the temptation to add a cherry!

EXOTIC FRUIT

Fruit in its various forms has always been with us and fortunately in this country, thanks to its colonial past, a whole myriad of tropical fruits have been known for centuries. Fruits like the banana are commonplace and hold no mystery for anyone. Sadly, though, I do feel many fruits like the banana are not used properly and tend to be treated as yet another addition to the fruit basket, to be eaten raw with very little thought as to how else they might be served. Certainly in the Caribbean, from where most of our bananas originate, they have all manner of delightful ways of serving bananas. I have included a recipe for just one such way in the hope that you will go on to consider the banana as more than just fresh fruit.

We are now beginning to see other exotic fruits more regularly in the high street, but I know from letters sent to me by viewers that many people are unsure of how to deal with them and so fight shy of bringing them home. Anyone can muster the skill to peel a banana but other fruits are a little more difficult. Take the pineapple for instance. There it sits, looking very grand with its crown of green spiky leaves, but where do you start with it? I wonder how many times a would-be pineapple purchaser has ended up reaching for a tin of pineapple chunks for the umpteenth time! Never fear, you too can meet a fresh pineapple on your home ground and despatch it with calculated skill. Once you have done one they'll hold no fear for you and you will see how useful a pineapple can be, especially as a pudding course. It is not too filling and its freshness of taste without all that sweet syrup you get with tinned pineapple is just right to clear the palate at the end of a meal.

There are other fruits, too, which are around like mangoes, lychees and kiwi fruit or chinese gooseberries as they are sometimes known. They will not always be the cheapest fruit available but they can really lift a meal either on their own or together. Which brings me to fruit salad. In this country fruit salad has been done a great disservice by the awful insipid tins of pretend fruit salad that are turned out in virtually every canteen you eat in. It is not unusual to find restaurants serving tinned fruit salad, and they really should know better. I know it takes more effort to cut up fresh fruit compared to opening a tin, but there really is no comparison between the two.

Pineapple

Pineapples come from various parts of the world – anywhere where it is hot enough and moist enough to grow them and that can extend from the West Indies to Israel. Most of them come from Hawaii. When you see them in the fields they look pretty forbidding; a great mass of spiky leaves looking for all the world like mini Triffids ready to slash you to ribbons and consume you if you come too close. Certainly the people who work with pineapples treat them with a healthy respect, wearing thick gloves to hold them as they slice the fruit from the ground with long machetes. When they arrive in the high streets of Britain they should be at their peak but nonetheless, as with all food buying, you should satisfy yourself that you are getting the right product. Look for a good head of leaves on the fruit, which should itself be unblemished by browning, and make sure also that the leaves are not seriously damaged. If many of the leaves have been torn or cut during transit it is possible the pineapple will have lost some of its moisture. Check the base of the fruit to see that it is intact – sometimes the fruit can be damaged by not being cut close enough to the ground. A ripe pineapple is bright orange in colour; any trace of green around the middle of the fruit shows it is not quite ready for eating.

Once you have taken the plunge and brought your pineapple home, how do you deal with it? There are a number of ways but the following two are the ones I have found most useful. The first is to make pineapple rings which can then be made into chunks if needed. It is perfectly acceptable to serve pineapple rings at a dinner party, as long as they are fresh. (I have almost the same view about pineapple as I have about tinned fruit salad.) Using a towel to protect your hands hold the pineapple by the leaves and cut off the bottom of the fruit so as to reveal a cut end of solid pineapple. You have to throw away the bottom bit or give it to a youngster to suck. Next cut the pineapple into slices about half to three-quarters of an inch thick. Using a sharp knife cut off the outside peel of each slice. Running down the centre of every pineapple is a central core of pith which has to be removed. If you are served with fresh pineapple at a posh restaurant the waiter will do this very deftly by spearing the slice in the centre with two forks and then cutting out the core with a sharp knife. I suggest you use a pastry cutter of suitable size – it's much quicker and easier. Arrange the slices on a serving plate and do not forget to use the top slice with all the leaves as a garnish. It looks good and apart from anything else it shows the pineapple was fresh – after all that trouble you don't want some insensitive person to think you've simply opened a tin!

Another way of serving pineapple is as boats, which is very attractive but perhaps a little more difficult to do. In effect you treat a pineapple as a melon, cutting it into wedges for individual servings. A reasonable pineapple will serve six people, a small one four. Stand the fruit the right way up and with a very sharp knife cut it in half lengthways. Now cut the two halves into two or three wedges, again lengthways. Some people prefer to use serrated knives – a bread knife is often very effective. Hold each wedge by the leaves and cut out the core of pith. Now cut as near to the skin as possible along the length of the wedge as you would with a melon. Next cut the wedge crossways to form segments. The wedge is now ready for serving. If you want to be really clever you can pull out each alternate segment on each wedge to provide a castellated look. Please, please, please, resist the temptation to put a cherry on the top of each wedge! If you are not serving pineapple immediately, it will benefit from being chilled before serving.

Mangoes
Mangoes are a far more perishable fruit than most which are imported into this country and like bananas they start to

ripen as soon as they are picked no matter how early the picking is done. However, unlike bananas no one has really adequately come up with a technique of slowing the ripening process in mangoes and as a result they have to be air freighted to this country from places like the Indian sub-continent which makes them relatively expensive. On top of all that, mangoes bruise very easily and once here they really only have a shelf life of about two days at the most. Of course there are tinned mangoes but as with other tinned fruit it really is not the same. So if you can find good fresh mangoes do buy them, as only then will you sample what is a truly exotic delight – the exquisite perfume of a mango. For me, this is almost as good as eating the fruit!

Mangoes come in a number of varieties. They can be green or yellow, some of them almost red in colour. You can tell how ripe they are by the feel of them rather than by the way they look. They should be firm but not hard. In the Indian sub-continent people talk about 'cutting' mangoes and 'sucking' mangoes. The 'cutting' mangoes tend to be larger, up to a foot in length, and are very firm. The 'sucking' mangoes are usually smaller and softer. The techniques for dealing with the two types are totally different.

Let us deal with cutting mangoes first. One large mango will provide enough for two people. Choose one that is firm. Mangoes have large flat stones which are difficult, but not impossible, to remove. The skill is to remove the stone without bringing with it too much of the fruit's flesh. Stand the mango on end and with a sharp knife cut as thick a slice as you can down the length of the mango. As you cut you will encounter the flat side of the stone. Cut the slice away and repeat for the other side of the mango. You now have two slices and a central section containing the stone. Cut around the section to remove the stone. The stone is quite hairy and inevitably you will seem to lose a lot of the mango flesh but there really is no way of avoiding this. Serve one slice to each person together with a share of the fruit from the middle section. If you like you can remove the skin from the mango before serving but I prefer to leave it on as it keeps the fruit in shape.

'Sucking' mangoes are much easier and much more fun to eat. You need one per person and they should be well ripe. Invite your guests to take a mango and gently soften it up by squeezing the fruit until it feels pulpy inside. During this process someone inevitably bursts his mango and there is an almighty mess. However, if it is done the right way the next stage is to bite off one end of the fruit and suck out the pulp and juice. When the stone is removed it is sucked clear of as much flesh as possible and then it only remains for the skin to be relieved of fruit. Sucking mangoes is messy to say the least but it provides an interesting end to a meal!

Lychees and Kiwi Fruit

Lychees were first introduced to this country in tinned form but it is now possible to get them fresh. I think they are best served unpeeled as they are simple to peel, the dark skin coming away quite cleanly from the fruit, as indeed does the small glossy stone in the centre of each fruit. Kiwi fruit, or Chinese gooseberries as they are sometimes called, are a little different. They contain small black pips which are eaten with the fruit. Kiwi fruit is best, I think, when used to garnish a fruit gateau or in a fruit salad. Peel off the hard brown skin, then cut the fruit crossways into thick slices.

A Proper Fruit Salad *(Serves 4)*

The success of any fruit salad depends on the preparation, not so much on the kind of fruit you put in, although of course that matters too. It is important to cut up the fruit into sizes and shapes appropriate to the texture of the fruit. One of the reasons I am so against tinned fruit salad is that everything seems to be cut up far too small and uniformly into the same boring cube shapes. This recipe suggests certain fruits, but vary them according to what is available.

1 large apple
1 pear
1 orange
1 banana
4 oz grapes

½ lb strawberries
½ fresh pineapple
1 lemon
1 tbsp brandy

Cut the apple into quarters and remove the core. Slice the apple very thinly. There is no need to peel the apple but make sure you do not include any bruised or damaged fruit. Do the same with the pear. Peel the orange and remove as much white pith as possible from the fruit. Cut the orange into large chunks, none smaller than an inch across. Peel the banana and cut it into slices. Halve the grapes and remove the pips. Hull the strawberries and cut them lengthwise in half. Cut the pineapple into chunks after removing the core and peel as explained on p. 54. Put all the fruit together in a large bowl and mix well but gently so as not to turn the whole thing into a pulp. Squeeze over the fruit salad the juice of the lemon and pour over the brandy. Chill well before serving. I find the taste of a fresh fruit salad is really brought out if you sprinkle black pepper over it, but perhaps this a personal preference and something you ought to let your guests decide for themselves!

Baked Bananas with Honey *(Serves 4)*

This really does make a change from the traditional way of eating bananas. It makes a good pudding and is also very good for serving at barbecues as the bananas can be prepared in advance and cooked in their foil parcels in the ashes.

4 bananas	*$\frac{1}{2}$ tsp cinnamon*
1 large orange	*2 oz brown sugar*
2 tbsp honey	*2 tbsp dark rum*

Peel the bananas making sure to remove any strings from the fruit. Lay each banana in its own piece of aluminium foil big enough to completely wrap the banana into a loose, sealed parcel. In a small saucepan heat up the honey so it becomes liquid but do not allow it to boil. Squeeze the juice from the orange and add it to the cinnamon mixing in well. Pour the cinnamon juice into the saucepan and stir in the brown sugar. Once it has all dissolved, remove from the heat and add the rum. Spoon the mixture over the bananas and seal up each foil parcel. Bake in a moderate oven, gas mark 5, 375°F, for twenty minutes to half an hour – until the bananas are tender. Serve in the foil to keep the juices.

STEAKS AND CHOPS

A well–cooked piece of meat whether it be steak or a chop is one of the easiest dishes to prepare in a hurry. The trouble is too many people use over–elaborate recipes and then end up spoiling the meat by losing it in too much flavour and too much cooking. I am convinced that with the high standard of meat we are blessed with in this country there is no need to go in for complicated cooking. That is not to say, though, that it is not necessary to understand the fundamentals of what meat is all about. The first thing to remember is that coming from an animal of one sort or another it varies tremendously with the type of animal and the age of the animal. Also, by the time it reaches you most meat has been through a number of processes. These days virtually all meat is frozen within minutes of the animal being slaughtered. In the old days meat used to be hung. This had the effect of allowing the meat to tenderise naturally. Meat that has been blast frozen will simply not be as tender and this has to be remembered when it comes to the cooking. Having said that, when you buy meat it is thawed out. So what do you look for? Let us take steaks first of all. There are various cuts of steak, but let us consider the two extremes: fillet and rump. Fillet is supposed to be more tender and so is more expensive, rump on the other hand is supposed to be tougher and so is cheaper. For my money I prefer rump steak because it is tastier and I know that, by and large, I can tenderise it myself before cooking. I save money, but there is another reason why I buy rump; there is usually more fat on a piece of rump steak. I know people have a thing about fat. They simply do not like it. This has led to our farmers striving to produce leaner animals, but often when you lose fat you lose flavour, so I like to see fat on a piece of meat. I also like to taste a well-cooked piece of fat, but even if you cut the fat off the meat, it can tell you quite a lot about the meat when you buy it. Generally speaking a good piece of steak should be bright red, possibly with a bluish tinge if the meat is particularly fresh, but if the meat looks at all grey and dowdy do not buy it. The fat on a good piece of meat should be bright white in colour; if it is overly yellow in colour the meat is past its best. Some of the best steak is 'marbled' with thin veins of fat running through it, which all helps in the tenderising when you come to cook the steak.

Much the same goes for chops, except there is always the bone to be considered. I always feel that most chops are too small to start with, and by the time you have cooked them and then taken the bone into account, it is hard to imagine why you bothered with chops in the first place! Nonetheless, the presence of the bone makes for better meat (the nearer the bone the sweeter the meat, etc), but do make sure the chops are big enough. If in doubt serve two (or even three) per person. The same rules apply about the meat being bright and glossy and the same goes for fat. In general pork chops seem to be much more generous as far as meat goes compared with lamb chops. Once you have chosen your meat there are any number of ways of cooking it but it all starts with tenderisation.

All meat is made up of fibres and when you tenderise the meat you are breaking down these fibres. This can be done in two ways, chemically or physically. The chemical way is not as frightening as it sounds but involves the use of marinades based on vinegar and oil such as the one described in the kebab section. Marinades are very effective but they take time to work. The physical method of tenderising is nothing like as subtle but it works instantly. You simply bash the meat for a good while and that breaks up the fibres. With steak and chops the best way to do this is to flatten it with one of those corrugated hammers made out of wood or metal. I prefer to use a wooden one. If you do not have one of these implements, a milk bottle serves just as well as long as you do not go at it too hard. Be careful too of the bone in the chops. It is possible to flatten a piece of steak to half its original thickness. This makes it easier to cook as the heat penetrates the steak more quickly. Once you have flattened your meat, it is ready for cooking by either frying or grilling. Grilling is slower and safer if you still have doubts about the tenderness of your meat, frying is quicker but then you top up the cholesterol level by adding more butter or oil. Whichever way you choose the meat must be seasoned, and the best way to do this is with what I call a herb sprinkle.

Herb Sprinkle

The whole idea of this is to bring out the flavour of the meat, not swamp it. The herbs given are the ones I generally use but you do not by any means need all of them and you can use different herbs if you prefer. If you have fresh herbs so much the better but dried herbs will do almost as well. You will see the recipe includes garlic: omit it if you must but you will be missing a great deal!

1 tsp each chopped thyme,	*Black pepper*
sage, chives, parsley	*Salt*
½ tsp chopped basil	*½ lemon*
2 cloves garlic	

Having battered your meat rub it all over with the half lemon and then sprinkle it with salt and plenty of black pepper. Ideally this should be from a pepper mill. Mix the herbs together and sprinkle over the meat using half the herbs. Peel and chop the garlic and sprinkle half of it over the meat. With dry hands press the herbs into the meat and then cook it. If you are frying, put the meat in the pan (in melted butter) herb side down. If you are grilling your meat, then put it under the grill herb side up. When you come to turn the meat sprinkle the rest of the herbs and garlic, not forgetting some more salt and pepper, on the other side.

Steak au Poivre *(Serves 2)*

This is just one of the many ways of cooking steak that has been made popular by the better restaurant. It happens to be my favourite; as you might have gathered by now I prefer things with a little bite to them. *Steak au poivre* does not need to be hot: you can use green peppercorns instead of the black ones.

2–12 oz pieces rump steak
½ lemon
2 cloves garlic
Salt
2 tbsp peppercorns
2 tsp chopped chives

1 tsp each chopped thyme
   and parsley
4 oz butter
2 tbsp brandy
1 glass white wine
½ pint cream

Batter the steaks and rub them over with the lemon. Peel and slice the garlic and press it into the steaks. Crush the peppercorns by putting them into a stout paper bag and hitting them with a rolling pin. The idea is to get large pieces of pepper rather than finely ground pepper. Lightly salt the steaks and press in the crushed peppercorns. Sprinkle half the herbs over the steaks. Melt the butter in a deep frying pan and gently fry the steaks on both sides. If the pan is not big enough use half the butter for each steak and fry them separately. Once the steaks are cooked, add the brandy to flame them. If you have a gas stove this is rather more easily done by pulling the frying pan to one side and allowing the brandy to catch fire. If you have an electric cooker then you may have to use a match. Remove the steaks from the pan to allow the juices to drain back and put them into a warm oven. Now add the rest of the herbs and the wine. Bring to the boil and allow to bubble for about a minute. Reduce the heat and stir in the cream. Keep the heat just below boiling and stir for about two minutes until the mixture begins to thicken. Use a wooden spoon for this and make sure you scrape the sauce from the bottom of the pan to prevent it burning. Pour the pepper sauce over the steaks and serve.

Pork Chops in Mustard Sauce *(Serves 4)*

There has been a growing fashion in cooking to incorporate traditional seasonings usually taken as accompaniments to a dish into the dish itself. Hence the next two recipes. With pork, mustard has always been considered essential to counterbalance the inherent sweetness of the meat. The same goes with lamb and mint sauce. With the pork recipe try to use one of the large-grain mustards rather than the fiery yellow English variety. Not only is it more acceptable to those who do not like hot foods but the texture of such softer mustards gives body to the sauce.

4 large pork chops	1 medium onion
Salt	1 clove garlic
Black pepper	2 tbsp mustard
½ lemon	1 tbsp whisky
1 tbsp cooking oil	½ pint single cream
2 oz butter	

Batter the pork chops as described above. Rub them over with the half lemon and then the oil. Sprinkle each chop generously with salt and black pepper. Put on one side. It is a good idea to leave them overnight in the fridge to allow the oil and lemon juice to get to work. In a deep-sided frying pan melt the butter and fry each chop until it is uniformly brown on each side. The idea is to seal the meat rather than cook it completely at this stage. Put the chops to one side allowing as much of the fat and juices to drain back into the frying pan as possible. Peel the onion and garlic and chop them very finely. Put them both in the frying pan and cook until soft. Add a little more butter if necessary. Now add the mustard to the pan and stir in well. Reduce the heat and add the whisky and cream, stirring well. Cook for about three minutes. Check the sauce for seasoning. Put the chops in a warm casserole and pour over the sauce. Cover the casserole and cook for half an hour in a moderate oven, gas mark 4, 350°F, until tender.

Lamb Chops in Minted Sauce *(Serves 4)*
Note that this recipe calls for a minted sauce rather than mint sauce. We are looking for a rather more subtle flavour than the heavy-handed mint sauce one buys in jars these days with lashings of sugar and vinegar. For this reason it is essential to use fresh mint; dried mint just will not do for this recipe. Fresh mint is easy enough to come by. After all, once you have it established in your garden you will never get rid of it!

4 lamb chops	Salt
2 tbsp oil	Black pepper
Juice of half a lemon	2 handfuls fresh mint
1 clove garlic	1 tbsp honey
1 small onion	2 tbsp vinegar

Batter the chops as described above and rub them over with the oil. Do this in a large casserole and then squeeze in the lemon juice and add a good sprinkling of salt and black pepper. Peel the onion and garlic and cut it into very thin slices. Cover the casserole and leave overnight to marinate. Turn the chops from time to time to make sure they do not dry out. In a small saucepan heat up the honey so it becomes liquid and mix in the vinegar. Wine vinegar is best for this. Take the mint leaves and chop them fairly coarsely leaving a few for garnish. Add the chopped leaves to the saucepan and stir in. Pour this sauce over the chops in the casserole. Put the casserole into a moderate oven, gas mark 4, 350°F, and bake the chops for between forty-five minutes and an hour. Test for tenderness and seasoning, and serve with plenty of the sauce and a sprinkle of chopped mint leaves.

Real Hamburgers (Serves 4)

Hamburgers have suffered from a bit of a battering over the years in Britain. Again, this has been because of the manufacturers of processed foods not being faithful to the dish in its original form. A youngster who has never travelled outside this country could easily be forgiven for thinking that a hamburger is just a rather flat tasteless lump of stringy mince meat. That, by and large, is what we end up getting from the food manufacturers whether we buy our hamburgers frozen or in tins. What a revelation then to travel in the United States, the home of the hamburger, and discover that hamburgers are large and tasty, so much so that they form a large part of the American staple diet.

The following recipe really does depend on the quality of mince meat you put into it. Americans talk about minced beef for a good hamburger and that means not too much fat. The best plan is to mince your own. If you buy mince and it has too high a proportion of fat in it, your hamburger, however well made, will shrink away to nothing. In the States they serve hamburgers in sesame seed buns. You can get them from some bakers but failing that, any kind of bread cake will do. Whatever you use they really ought to be cut in half and toasted before filling with your hamburger.

2 lb mince	*1 tsp chopped sage*
1 medium onion	*1 tsp chopped thyme*
1 tsp black pepper	*1 egg*
1 tsp salt	*1 cup breadcrumbs*

Peel the onion and chop it, but not too finely. Mix it into the mince meat together with the herbs and spices. It is really best to use your hands for this. Break the egg into the mixture and mix it well in. Now add the breadcrumbs until the mince meat mixture feels dry to the touch. You will need more or less breadcrumbs depending on how much moisture they absorb. Divide the mixture into four equal parts and form into flat patty shapes at least an inch thick. You can either fry the hamburgers in a little butter or use the traditional method of grilling them (which the Americans call broiling). As you do this flatten the hamburgers slightly with a wooden spatula. Make sure they are well browned but do not overcook them otherwise they will shrink away to nothing. Serve in toasted buns with plenty of salt and tomato sauce, and whatever other dressings you can lay your hands on. Once you have made hamburgers yourself, you will never want to buy another frozen one!